MW00946249

the overdue fine is
.05 per day

MCO

GERMAN IMMIGRANTS

1820-1920

by Helen Frost

Content Consultant:
Don Heinrich Tolzmann, Ph.D.,
Curator of the German Americana Collection
and Director of the German American Studies Program,
University of Cincinnati,
Cincinnati, Ohio

Blue Earth Books

an imprint of Capstone Press
Mankato, Minnesota

Blue Earth Books are published by Capstone Press
151 Good Counsel Drive, P.O. Box 669, Mankato, Minnesota 56002
http://www.capstone-press.com

Library of Congress Cataloging-in-Publication Data
Frost, Helen, 1949–
    German immigrants, 1820–1920 / by Helen Frost.
    p. cm. — (Coming to America)
    Includes bibliographical references (p. 31) and index.
    ISBN 0-7368-0794-2
    1. German Americans—History—Juvenile literature. 2. Immigrants—United States—History—Juvenile literature. 3. United States—Emigration and
immigration—History—Juvenile literature. 4. Germany—Emigration and immigration—History—Juvenile literature. [1. German Americans—History
2. Immigrants—History. 3. United States—Emigration and immigration.] I. Title II. Coming to America (Mankato, Minn.)
    E184.G3 F875 2002
    973' .0431—dc21   00-013126

Summary: Discusses reasons German people left their homeland to come to America, the experiences immigrants had in the new country, and the contributions this cultural group made to American society. Includes sidebars and activities.

Editorial credits
Editor: Kay M. Olson
Designer: Heather Kindseth
Photo Researcher: Heidi Schoof
Product Planning Editor: Lois Wallentine

Photo credits
Fred Hultstrand History in Pictures Collection, NDIRS-NDSU, Fargo, ND, cover, 19; Minnesota Historical Society, 4, 12, 13 (top), 23; Gregg Andersen, flag images, 6, 13 (bottom), 25; North Wind Picture Archives, 7; Library of Congress, 8, 18, 20, 24; Bettmann/CORBIS, 9, 11, 15; Historical Picture Archive/CORBIS, 10; Robert Dennis Collection of Stereoscopic Views, The New York Public Library, 14; DeWitt Historical Society/Archive Photos, 16; Matt Sullivan/The (Fort Wayne, IN) Journal Gazette, 8/31/00, 17; Nat Fein/Archive Photos, 21; Tony Vaccaro/Archive Photos, 22; A. O. Buck, Minnesota Historical Society, 26 (top); AFP/CORBIS, 26 (bottom); Stock Montage, Inc., 29 (both)

2 3 4 5 6 07 06 05 04 03 02

Contents

EARLY GERMAN IMMIGRANTS

Germans made up the largest group of immigrants to come to the United States. But it is not always easy to say who should be counted as a German immigrant. During the early 1800s, people lived in many places in Europe where German was the common language. People who left these places to go to America are considered German immigrants. In 1871, many of these German-speaking areas were united as the country of Germany.

The largest number of German immigrants came to America in the late 1800s. But some Germans arrived much earlier. In 1683, a group of Germans started the community of Germantown in Pennsylvania. Other groups arrived in America in the 1700s and formed communities along the East Coast.

During the Revolutionary War (1775–1783), the British hired about 30,000 Hessians. Known as fierce fighters, these German soldiers were paid to help battle the American colonists. At least 6,000 Hessian soldiers deserted the English army and fought for the American colonists. After the war, about 12,000 Hessians stayed in America. Many of the Hessians became early U.S. citizens.

By 1790, the U.S. population had reached almost 4 million. Of that number, about 360,000 were German immigrants or their descendants. These early settlers established their own communities where everyone spoke German.

By 1820, large numbers of people started leaving German regions to come to America. Many were farmers seeking new land and a better life. Many German

Most early German immigrants were farmers or craftspeople. But some were merchants, intellectuals, artists, writers, scientists, lawyers, ministers, and teachers.

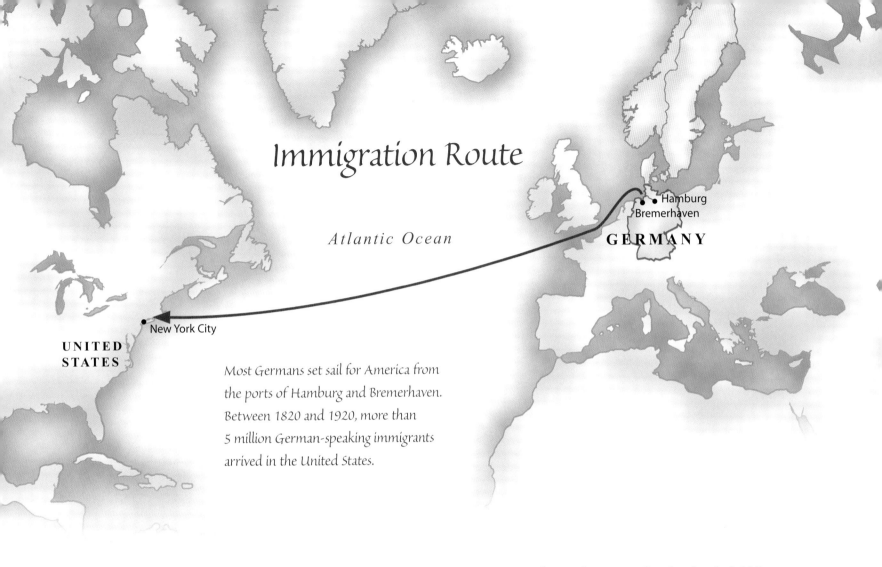

Immigration Route

Atlantic Ocean

GERMANY

● Hamburg
Bremerhaven

**UNITED
STATES**

● New York City

*Most Germans set sail for America from
the ports of Hamburg and Bremerhaven.
Between 1820 and 1920, more than
5 million German-speaking immigrants
arrived in the United States.*

immigrants came to America because they wanted to be free
to worship in their own way. Most German immigrants
found ways to make a living and stay in America.

Between 1820 and 1920, a total of 5,496,691 people
left Germany for America. The descendants of German
immigrants make up almost one-fourth of today's U.S.
population. More than 58 million Americans report having
German ancestry. This group of German Americans has
had a strong influence on U.S. culture. Their customs and
inventions play an important part in American life today.

LIFE IN THE OLD COUNTRY

Germans were skilled at a variety of crafts, including woodworking and clock making. The cuckoo clock comes from the Black Forest area of Germany.

In the early 1800s, there was no such thing as a typical German citizen. Germans practiced different religions and held a variety of occupations and skills. Some Germans could not read or write. But many others were talented musicians and writers who created important works. Some German families had lived in the same place for generations. Others had a strong "wanderlust," the desire to travel and seek out new places to live.

People living in the German-speaking regions shared a common culture. They ate foods such as pretzels, sausages, sauerkraut, and gingerbread. They told their children stories by the Brothers Grimm, such as "Hansel and Gretel," "The Bremen Town Musicians," and "Cinderella." Skilled German craftspeople made furniture, cuckoo clocks, and silverware. German families sang "Stille Nacht" (Silent Night) and "O Tannenbaum" (Oh Christmas Tree) as they decorated evergreen trees inside their homes at Christmastime.

The nobility, a small group of wealthy and powerful people, ruled the German peasants. The nobility owned land and collected high rents and taxes from the people who farmed it. The German nobility could force peasants to serve in their armies. But some people belonged to religious groups that opposed war and other forms of violence. They did not want to be soldiers.

Between 1820 and 1920, many people emigrated and left Germany to start a new life in America. People had to leave behind their families, friends, and familiar surroundings. America was a faraway and unfamiliar place.

The city of Hamburg in Germany is located on the Elbe River near its mouth in the North Sea. In the late 1800s, many Germans who came to America boarded ships that left from Hamburg's port.

Germans decided to emigrate for different reasons. Some left because there were more people in Germany than the land could support. Farmers and their families faced famine when crops failed. Other people were not willing to fight in the German army. Some Germans believed that the nobility had too much power and did not rule in a fair manner. In some regions, Catholics and Anabaptists wanted religious freedom from the Protestants in power. In regions where the Catholics were in power, Protestants wanted their own religious freedom.

Many Germans had heard wonderful stories about North America. Germans already living in America wrote letters to friends and relatives in Germany. They told about plentiful farmland that anyone could own. They explained that the U.S. government guaranteed everyone religious freedom. These letters encouraged other Germans to immigrate to America.

The first major wave of German immigrants came to the United States between 1820 and 1860. Historians use the term "wave" to describe large groups of immigrants who came to America during certain time periods. Between 1851 and 1860, almost 1 million German immigrants arrived in America. In 1854 alone, 215,000 people came to the United States from Germany. Many of these German immigrants were farmers and craftspeople.

In the late 1840s and early 1850s, a group called the 48ers came from Germany to America. These people took part in a revolution in Germany in 1848. They tried to unite Germany under a democratic form of government. When their revolution failed, about 5,000 of the 48ers left Germany and came to the United States.

Many 48ers were scientists, artists, writers, journalists, lawyers, ministers, and teachers. These immigrants contributed their knowledge and talent to America as teachers, politicians, publishers, religious leaders, and other

Carl Schurz was a well-known German immigrant who spoke out against slavery in the United States. He served as a Union general in the Civil War (1861–1865) and was a noted American journalist.

public figures. Carl and Margarethe Schurz were 48ers who immigrated to the United States in the 1800s. Carl worked closely with Abraham Lincoln and was an opponent of slavery who fought for the Union in the Civil War (1861–1865). Margarethe started the first kindergarten in America in 1856.

A German revolution started in the spring of 1848. Citizens in southern Germany demanded freedom of the press, trial by jury, and constitutional systems of government in all German states.

THE TRIP OVER

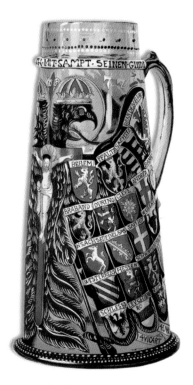

German drinking glasses are called steins. Immigrants often packed steins in the luggage they brought to America.

Families often did not have enough money to travel together from Germany to America. They usually sent the father or the oldest son first. He worked on a farm or in a trade, saved his earnings, and sent money to Germany. The rest of the family was then able to save enough money for the trip to America.

Those families with enough money could travel together. Sometimes an entire German community went to America as a group. This practice was especially common in religious communities. All members of one church would make the trip together and establish a new church in America.

Before they could emigrate, Germans had to have certain documents. No birth certificates were issued in the German region of Europe in the 1800s. Instead, people kept records of baptisms and marriages to prove who they were, where they had been born, and how old they were. Men needed proof that they had completed their German military service. If they had not served in the army, they had to pay a fee. In some German regions, emigrants had to pay a "leave tax" before they could leave.

When they had these travel documents, Germans had to save enough money for boat passage. They then had to decide what to take with them to America. People packed warm clothes and blankets, family Bibles, and teakettles. Some took small envelopes of dirt to remind them of their homeland. People often carried maps showing German settlements in America. The maps showed the American roads,

Early immigrants traveled from Germany to the United States on sailing ships. Later, immigrants arrived by steamships, which were faster and made the trip across the Atlantic Ocean in weeks rather than months.

11

In the mid-1800s, many Germans traveled by train to the ports of Bremerhaven or Hamburg in Germany. They then transferred to a ship to cross the Atlantic Ocean.

and the crowded bunks were full of bedbugs. Diseases often spread quickly in the crowded and unsanitary conditions. Head lice carried a disease called typhus, which caused high fevers and headaches. So many German immigrants became ill with typhus that the disease was sometimes called "Palatine Fever," named after a region of Germany.

Many immigrants made new friends during the trip to America. Steerage passengers could wander to the upper decks to get exercise and fresh air. They sometimes met people from other countries and began to learn new languages. Some young people became engaged on the ships and later married in the United States.

In the mid-1850s, steamships replaced sailing ships. Steamships could make the trip from Germany to America in two or three weeks. Built to carry passengers, these vessels were more comfortable for all travelers. By the early 1900s, large steamships traveled on regular schedules between Hamburg and New York City.

railroads, canals, and rivers that would guide new immigrants to the settlements.

Early emigrants traveled from Germany to the United States on ships. The trip took six weeks to three months. The steerage section of the boat carried cargo to America, but it was rarely full. Most of the German immigrants did not have enough money to pay for a private room on the ship, so they traveled in the cheaper steerage section with the cargo.

Conditions in the steerage section were miserable. The drinking water was not fresh. Water was stored in barrels for weeks and it often smelled and tasted terrible. Many people became seasick. The steerage section often was full of rats,

★ Packing to Leave ★

What you need

> paper and pencil
>
> a small box or suitcase

What you do

1. Imagine that you are leaving home to go to a new country. You are allowed to take only one small box or suitcase.

2. With paper and pencil, make a list of what you want to take with you.

3. Gather the items on your list.

4. Try to arrange everything so it all fits in your box or suitcase.

5. If everything does not fit, decide what you will leave behind.

6. Ask your friends and family what they would take, and compare their lists with yours. Talk about why you decided to bring the items on your lists.

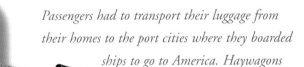

Passengers had to transport their luggage from their homes to the port cities where they boarded ships to go to America. Haywagons piled with suitcases, boxes, and baskets were a common sight in many German cities during the late 1800s. Children were able to bring only as much as they could carry by themselves.

ARRIVING IN AMERICA

Castle Garden was the first stop for most new immigrants between 1855 and 1890. This examining and processing center was later replaced by the one on Ellis Island.

German immigrants who entered the United States usually arrived in New York City. Beginning in 1855, immigrants and their luggage were checked at New York's Castle Garden. But by 1890, the U.S. government needed a larger facility to handle the increasing number of immigrants from all over the world. In 1892, Ellis Island opened in New York Harbor and became the first stop in America for most German immigrants. Other Germans entered America through ports in Baltimore, Philadelphia, and New Orleans.

Immigrants had to pass through an inspection at Castle Garden or Ellis Island before they were allowed to enter the country. Customs inspectors examined each immigrant, looking for contagious diseases. They checked people's eyes, throats, ears, and skin for signs of infection. They also asked questions to find out whether the immigrants could speak English, had job skills, and would be good U.S. citizens.

Many immigrants were frightened by the inspection. They saw the inspectors using a sharp, hook-shaped tool called a buttonhook to check people's eyes for an infection called trachoma. Immigrants could not enter the country if they were not healthy enough to pass the examination. Parents who had sick children worried that they would have to leave their young sons or daughters behind at the Ellis Island hospital until they were well. Inspectors sometimes sent very sick immigrants back to their homeland.

Doctors inspected each arriving immigrant for signs of sickness or disease. The U.S. government wanted to make sure that immigrants were healthy enough to work and support themselves in America.

Two out of every 100 immigrants were not allowed to enter the United States. The shipping companies had to take those people back to their homeland, free of charge. But sometimes one family member passed the inspection and another did not. The shipping company did not have to give free passage back home to those who were allowed into the United States. Families sometimes were split when one person was sent back home, and the rest of the family was allowed to stay.

Immigrants who passed through the inspection points faced other obstacles as they started their new lives in America. They had to find their way around in a country that was bigger than Germany, but did not have as many roads and trains. They had to find a place to live and a way to earn money. They had to avoid being tricked by people who wanted to cheat them or steal from them.

Friends and relatives often were waiting for the new immigrants when they arrived. The Germans who had been in the United States for a while could help new immigrants get settled. In some cities, Immigrant Aid Societies helped newcomers who did not have family or friends to meet them.

About half of the German immigrants stayed in the cities where they first arrived. New York, Baltimore, Philadelphia, and New Orleans became home to large German American communities. Families often lived in crowded tenement buildings. Other Germans traveled to cities north of the Ohio River, such as Cincinnati, St. Louis, Chicago, and Milwaukee. German settlements were already well established in these cities. Some of the new arrivals stayed with friends or relatives. Others lived in boarding houses.

Many German immigrants who had been farmers in their homeland went to live in farm communities in the Upper Midwest. States bordering the Great Lakes had many large German settlements. By the mid-1800s, Wisconsin and Minnesota were the most German of all the U.S. states.

As the immigrants settled in cities and rural areas, they started German newspapers, schools, and churches. German Americans became skilled workers, farmers, laborers, teachers, musicians, and artists. German culture became an important part of life in the United States.

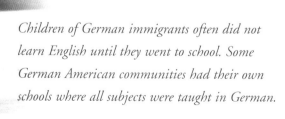

Children of German immigrants often did not learn English until they went to school. Some German American communities had their own schools where all subjects were taught in German.

16

★ Papierschnitt ★

German parents and grandparents entertained children on the voyage to America and during the wait at Castle Garden or Ellis Island. One favorite activity was papierschnitt, or paper folding and cutting. Folding and cutting paper to make paper snowflakes is one form of papierschnitt.

Another method of paper folding makes a chain of figures when the paper is cut and unfolded. If the figures are people, they look like little dolls, each holding the hand of the other. It was easy for German immigrants to entertain children with this craft because it requires simple materials such as paper and scissors. You can make your own papierschnitt chain of people, animals, or other shapes.

What You Need

paper

pencil

scissors

crayons or colored
  markers (optional)

This Twelve Days of Christmas papierschnitt was created by Connie Squires.

What You Do

1. Cut a strip of paper about 11 inches (28 centimeters) long and 2 inches (5 centimeters) wide. The chain will be as long and wide as the paper you use.

2. Fold the paper in half, then fold in half again, and then in half again. Make creases along each fold.

3. Open the paper, smooth it flat, and fold it again along the creases. This time, fold it like an accordion. Every other fold should be on the opposite side.

4. Draw a figure such as a heart, a person, or a tree on the top of the folded paper. Some point of the figure should touch each folded side.

5. Cut carefully along the figure you have drawn.

6. Open the paper. Your figures should be in a chain.

7. Use crayons or colored markers to color your figures, if you wish.

SURVIVING IN AMERICA

Barges along the Erie Canal carried many German immigrants from New York to the Midwest. They traveled on barges along the Hudson River and through the Erie Canal to the Great Lakes. Many Germans headed to the Upper Midwest region to stake their claims for farmland under the Homestead Act.

From port cities, many German immigrants traveled to the farmland and industrial cities of the Upper Midwest. Immigrants who arrived at the eastern seaports usually traveled inland by wagon or train, or along rivers and canals. Those who entered the country in New Orleans took riverboats up the Mississippi River to settlements north of the Ohio River. So many German immigrants settled near the three cities of Milwaukee, Cincinnati, and St. Louis that the area became known as the German Triangle. Many Germans also settled in the states of Minnesota and Wisconsin.

From 1817 to 1835, German immigrants were hired to help build the Erie Canal. This channel provided a water passage from Albany to Buffalo in Upstate New York. Combined with the Hudson River, the canal allowed ships to travel between the Atlantic Ocean and the Great Lakes. The Erie Canal made it easier for Germans and other immigrants to travel to cities, small towns, and farmlands along the Great Lakes.

Some German settlements were Catholic, Lutheran, or Jewish. Other groups formed Mennonite, Amish, Hutterite, or Quaker communities. Many of these groups used the German language in church services well into the 1900s. German is still the primary language spoken in some Amish and Hutterite communities today.

German immigrants helped one another with farm chores such as threshing wheat and stacking hay.

Life in the United States was not as easy as many German immigrants expected it to be. Some immigrants had heard that American streets were paved with gold. When they arrived, they saw that the cities were still being built. Few roads were paved at all. German farmers heard about wide-open empty spaces in the American west. But farmland had to be cleared and planted. Making a living in America took a lot of hard work and determination.

Despite hardships, most German immigrants adapted well to life in America. Only about one of every eight German immigrants returned to Germany. Some were homesick; some had no jobs or money. A few went back to marry the sweethearts they had left behind. The rest stayed, found a way to make a living, and became U.S. citizens.

German immigrants were more highly skilled than most other immigrant groups. More than half were skilled

Some German Americans opened grocery stores and other businesses. Midwestern towns quickly grew during the second half of the 1800s, when new immigrants arrived daily.

laborers, with work experience in carpentry, clock making, paper making, coach building, and other crafts. Many German immigrants used these skills to establish successful small businesses.

Other German immigrants were farmers. They were used to working hard on their farms in Germany, and they were willing to keep working hard in the United States. In 1862, Congress passed the Homestead Act. This law allowed many German Americans to stake a claim for a piece of farmland. The head of a family could claim 160 acres of public land. After the family cleared the land and lived on it for five years, they owned it.

Some German immigrants expanded their small farms into large factories. Many meat-packing, food-processing, and baking factories were started by German immigrants. Other German immigrants worked in the brewing industry and in logging and paper mills.

Education and culture were important to many German immigrants. Thousands of small singing societies sprang up in German communities. German immigrants started schools, universities, and symphony orchestras. They started hundreds of German-language newspapers and journals.

By the late 1800s, the German communities in America were well-established. New immigrants started to arrive in large numbers from Italy, Russia, and other countries. The Germans became known as "Old Immigrants," because so many of them had been in the United States for a long time.

Serious problems arose for German Americans during World War I (1914–1918), when the United States was at war with Germany. Some Americans questioned the loyalty of German American citizens.

Many German Americans stopped speaking German and participating in German cultural activities. Some changed their names to make them sound more English.

By 1920, many things that people thought of as "All American" were actually German in origin. For example, frankfurters were sausages named after a city in Germany. Americans started calling the spicy sausages "hot dogs," and they became a popular food. Although names were changed, the German influence on American life continued to be important.

German American Language

Some German words are very much a part of the American English language today. Did you know:

the word	we use to mean	in German really means
dachshund	a type of dog	badger hunter
Gesundheit	God bless you	good health to you
hamburger	meat patty on a bun	someone from Hamburg, Germany
kindergarten	the grade before first grade	children's garden
sauerkraut	relish for a hot dog	sour cabbage
frankfurter	hot dog	someone from Frankfurt, Germany

KEEPING TRADITIONS

German immigrants introduced accordion music to America.

The descendants of German immigrants make up a large portion of the U.S. population today. More than 58 million Americans claim some German background. When Americans go on a picnic and eat hamburgers or hot dogs, they are enjoying German foods. When children look for Easter eggs or decorate a Christmas tree, they are sharing old German customs. When they listen to fairy tales, such as "Little Red Riding Hood" or "Rumpelstiltskin," they are learning stories that have been passed down from German ancestors.

About 750,000 German Americans fought for the Union in the Civil War. But others continued to oppose military service. They found other ways to serve their country. Some worked as hospital orderlies, caring for wounded soldiers. Others raised money for food and supplies for the troops.

German immigrants had a strong influence on American education. Margarethe Meyer Schurz started the first kindergarten in America. The practice of giving young children a year of learning before entering first grade spread throughout the country. Other German American educators started universities and schools that were similar to those they had known in Germany. German Americans introduced gymnastics and physical education to American schools.

German immigrants celebrated their German heritage with parades, foods, songs, and customs from their homeland. Many of these celebrations and customs have become a part of American life for all citizens.

American journalists were greatly influenced by the traditions of German American news writers. From 1850 to 1900, hundreds of German-language newspapers flourished in American cities. Anna Ottendoerfer, a German immigrant, was editor and manager of the *New-Yorker Staats-Zeitung*. It became one of the most widely-read German newspapers in America.

In the mid-1800s, German musicians dominated music in the United States. The symphony orchestras in Philadelphia, New York City, and Boston were all started by German immigrants. Most of the musicians were German Americans, and much of the music they played was written by German composers, such as Ludwig van Beethoven, Johann Sebastian Bach, and Richard Wagner. Choir groups were still popular in many German communities.

As the United States expanded westward, people hired German craftspeople to build homes and cities. German American parents taught their crafts to their children, and the same business sometimes stayed in one family for generations. For example, Henry Engelhard Steinweg started

The Amish and similar religious groups continue to follow the dress and customs of early German immigrants. They travel in horse-drawn wagons and rely on the farming practices of the 1800s.

making pianos in his kitchen in Germany. He and his children continued to make pianos in the United States. The company they started, Steinway & Sons, still makes pianos today.

In traditional German families, women stayed home to take care of the house and children. They also devoted time to the community and volunteered in hospitals and orphanages. Some women worked outside the home if the family needed their income. Others took in "piece work."

These women worked at home, sewing garments as quickly as they could. Their employers paid them according to the number of finished garments they made.

In some places in America, the descendants of German immigrants still continue to practice their religious and cultural traditions. People in Amish communities speak German, drive horse-drawn buggies, and dress in a plain style, much as their ancestors did when they first came to America.

★ Pfeffernuesse ★

What You Need

Ingredients:

2¼ cups (550 mL) flour

½ teaspoon (2 mL) each: salt, ground black pepper, anise seed, and ground cinnamon

¼ teaspoon (1 mL) each: baking soda, ground allspice, and ground nutmeg

⅛ teaspoon (.5 mL) ground cloves

½ cup (125 mL) softened butter

1 cup (250 mL) light brown sugar

¼ cup (50 mL) light molasses

1 egg

1 cup (250 mL) powdered sugar (for dusting cookies)

Equipment:

two mixing bowls

wooden spoon

measuring cups

measuring spoons

electric mixer

baking sheets

pot holders

sturdy paper bag

wire cooling racks

Pfeffernuesse cookies are a traditional German cookie. They have a sharp ginger and pepper flavor.

What You Do

1. In one bowl, use a wooden spoon to mix together flour, salt, pepper, anise seed, ground cinnamon, baking soda, allspice, nutmeg, and cloves.

2. In the other bowl, combine butter, brown sugar, and light molasses. Using the electric mixer, mix ingredients for about 4 minutes on medium speed, until the mixture is light and fluffy.

3. Mix in one egg.

4. Set the mixer speed to low. Add the flour mixture about ½ cup (125 mL) at a time, mixing after each addition.

5. Cover the dough and refrigerate 2 or 3 hours.

6. Roll the dough into balls about the size of a walnut and place on the baking sheet 2 inches (5 centimeters) apart.

7. Preheat the oven to 350°F (180°C). Bake for 15 minutes.

8. Let the cookies cool a little, but do not let them get cold.

9. Put the powdered sugar into the paper bag.

10. Take the cookies off the cookie sheets and drop them into the bag, a few at a time. Shake the bag gently to coat the cookies with sugar.

11. Put the cookies on the cooling racks until they are completely cool.

Makes about 30 cookies

German Americans now live all across America. The largest number of German Americans live in the Midwest. German customs and traditions have blended well into American society and have become part of the mainstream culture. Most German Americans now speak English. They take pride in their German heritage as well as the contributions made by their German immigrant ancestors.

From the early to the late 1900s, many proud German Americans have celebrated their heritage by decorating floats and participating in German festivals, parades, and parties. German American Day is celebrated on October 6 in the United States. This special day honors the founding of Germantown, Pennsylvania, on this date in 1683.

★ Make a Family Tree ★

Genealogy is the study of family history. Genealogists often record this history in the form of a family tree. This chart records a person's ancestors, such as parents, grandparents, and great-grandparents.

Start your own family tree with the names of your parents and grandparents. Ask family members for their full names, including their middle names. Remember that your mother and grandmothers likely had a different last name before they were married. This name, called a maiden name, probably is the same as their fathers' last name.

Making a family tree helps you to know your ancestors and the countries from which they emigrated. Some people include the dates and places of birth with each name on their family tree. Knowing when and where these relatives were born will help you understand from which immigrant groups you have descended.

There are many ways to find information for your family tree. Ask for information from your parents, grandparents, and as many other older members of your family as you can. Some people research official birth and death records to find the full names of relatives. Genealogical societies often have information that will help with family tree research. If you know the cemetery where family members are buried, you may find some of the information you need on the gravestones.

Your father's mother

Your mother's father

Your father's father

Your mother's mother

Your father

Your mother

You

★ TIMELINE ★

1829
Gottfried Duden publishes a book about his farming experiences in Missouri. The book is distributed in Germany. Many Germans, encouraged by his positive descriptions, decide to emigrate.

1848
A revolution fails in Germany. About 5,000 48ers emigrate to America during the early 1850s.

1854
215,000 German immigrants come to the United States in one year.

1862
The Homestead Act is passed. Many immigrants move west to claim farmland.

1873
Levi Strauss & Co. patents blue jeans.

1882
About 250,000 German immigrants arrive in the United States, more than in any other year.

1920
German American Albert Einstein wins the Nobel Prize in physics.

1800

1900

1820
The United States begins officially counting the number of immigrants.

1847
Hamburg-America Shipping Company is founded, specializing in transporting passengers instead of cargo.

1861–1865
The Northern states and Southern states fight the Civil War.

1877
German American Carl Schurz is named Secretary of the Interior.

1917
The United States enters World War I and fights against Germany as well as other countries.

1860
About 200 German-language newspapers are published in the United States.

★ **Sandra Bullock** (1964–) Born in Washington, D.C., Bullock is the daughter of German opera singer Helga Meyer and American voice coach John Bullock. She is a TV and movie actress. One of her best-known roles is Annie Porter in the movie *Speed*.

★ **Albert Einstein** (1879–1955) Born in Ulm, Germany, Einstein was one of the most important scientists of the 1900s. His Theory of Relativity and work in physics, mathematics, and philosophy are considered works of genius.

★ **Dwight D. Eisenhower** (1890–1961) Born in Denison, Texas, Eisenhower was brought up in Abilene, Kansas. He was third in a family of seven sons of a third-generation German immigrant family. On D-Day in 1944, Eisenhower was Supreme Commander of the allied troops who invaded France. He was elected the 34th U.S. president and served in this office from 1953 to 1961.

Albert Einstein

★ **Henry J. Heinz** (1844–1919) Born in Pittsburgh, Pennsylvania, Heinz's family descended from German immigrants. He founded the H. J. Heinz Company, which manufactures pickles, spices, relishes, and other foods.

★ **Herbert Hoover** (1874–1964) Hoover was the son of a German Quaker blacksmith. In 1927, he became the first German American U.S. president.

★ **George Herman "Babe" Ruth** (1895–1948) The son of German immigrants, Babe Ruth was the best-known baseball player of the 1920s. He hit 714 home runs during his baseball career.

Babe Ruth

Words to Know

ancestry (AN-sess-tree)—a person's family members who lived long ago, usually before one's grandparents

Amish (AH-mish)—members of the strict Anabaptist religious group that in 1693 broke away to follow Joseph Amman

contagious (kuhn-TAY-juhss)—a contagious disease is spread by direct contact with someone or something already infected with it

descendant (di-SEND-uhnt)—a person's child and the generations of a family born after that child

emigrate (EM-uh-grate)—to leave your own country in order to live in another one

48er (for-ti-AY-tur)—a person who came to America after the 1848 revolution in Germany failed; about 5,000 German Americans were 48ers.

Homestead Act (HOM-sted AKT)—an act passed by Congress in 1862 that allowed a person to claim a 160-acre (65-hectare) piece of public land; the person had to clear and improve the land and live on it for five years in order to own it.

Hutterite (HUHT-ur-ite)—a member of a certain religious group that lives together, dresses in similar clothing, shares possessions, and owns common property

immigrant (IM-uh-gruhnt)—someone who comes from another country to live permanently in a new one

Mennonite (MEN-uhn-ite)—a member of an independent religious group especially known for rejecting military service

Quaker (KWAY-kur)—a member of the Society of Friends; this Christian group founded in 1650 is opposed to war.

stein (STYN)—a drinking glass or mug with a handle and sometimes a cover that opens and closes

wanderlust (WAHN-dur-lust)—desire to travel; some Germans were noted for their wanderlust.

To Learn More

Collier, Christopher, and James Lincoln Collier. *A Century of Immigration: 1820–1924.* Drama of American History. New York: Marshall Cavendish/Benchmark Books, 1999.

Fahey, Kathleen. *The Germans.* We Came to North America. New York: Crabtree Publishing, 2001.

Hoobler, Dorothy, and Thomas Hoobler. *The German American Family Album.* American Family Albums. New York: Oxford University Press, 1995.

Schouweiler, Tom. *Germans in America.* In America. Minneapolis: Lerner Publications, 1994.

Shnidman, Ellen. *The German-American Answer Book.* Ethnic Answer Books. Philadelphia: Chelsea House, 1999.

Places to Write and Visit

American Historical Society of Germans from Russia
631 D Street
Lincoln, NE 68502-1199

Deutscheim State Historic Site
109 West Second Street
Hermann, MO 65041

Ellis Island Library
Statue of Liberty National Monument
One Liberty Island
New York, NY 10004-1467

Germanic-American Institute
301 Summit Avenue
St. Paul, MN 55102-2118

Indiana German Heritage Society
401 East Michigan Street
Indianapolis, IN 46204

Pennsylvania German Cultural Heritage Center
Weisenberger Alumni Center
Kutztown University
Kutztown, PA 19530

Internet Sites

Ellis Island
http://www.ellisisland.org

German-Americana Collection at the University of Cincinnati
http://www.archives.uc.edu/german

German American Day
http://www3.serve.com/shea/germusa/usafrg.htm

German American Historic Sites and Museums
http://www-lib.iupui.edu/kade/gahist.html

German American History and Heritage
http://www.germanheritage.com

Germans in America—Chronology (Library of Congress)
http://www.loc.gov/rr/european/imde/germchro.html

Index